M000083858

What Is Faith?

Basics of the Faith

How Do We Glorify God?

How Our Children Come to Faith

What Are Election and Predestination?

What Are Spiritual Gifts?

What Is a Reformed Church?

What Is a True Calvinist?

What Is Biblical Preaching?

What Is Church Government?

What Is Discipleship?

What Is Faith?

What Is Grace?

What Is Hell?

What Is Justification by Faith Alone?

What Is Man?

What Is Perseverance of the Saints?

What Is Providence?

What Is Spiritual Warfare?

What Is the Atonement?

What Is the Christian Worldview?

What Is the Doctrine of Adoption?

What Is the Lord's Supper?

What Is the Trinity?

What Is True Conversion?

What Is Vocation?

What Is Worship Music?

Why Believe in God?

Why Do We Baptize Infants?

Why Do We Have Creeds?

Why Do We Pray?

Why God Gave Us a Book

Sean Michael Lucas, Series Editor

What Is Faith?

Guy M. Richard

P&R
PUBLISHING
P.O. BOX 817 • PHILLIPSBURG • NEW JERSEY 08865-0817

© 2012 by Guy M. Richard

All rights reserved. No part of this book may be reproduced, stored in a retrieval system, or transmitted in any form or by any means—electronic, mechanical, photocopy, recording, or otherwise—except for brief quotations for the purpose of review or comment, without the prior permission of the publisher, P&R Publishing Company, P.O. Box 817, Phillipsburg, New Jersey 08865-0817.

Unless otherwise indicated, Scripture quotations are from The Holy Bible, English Standard Version, copyright © 2001 by Crossway Bibles, a division of Good News Publishers. Used by permission. All rights reserved.

ISBN: 978-1-59638-430-9 (pbk)
ISBN: 978-1-59638-554-2 (ePub)
ISBN: 978-1-59638-553-5 (Mobi)

The passage from *He Is There and He Is Not Silent* by Francis Schaeffer is used by permission of Tyndale House Publishers, Inc. Copyright © 1972 by Francis A. Schaeffer. All rights reserved.

Page design by Tobias Design

Printed in the United States of America

Library of Congress Cataloging-in-Publication Data

Richard, Guy M.
  What is faith? / Guy M. Richard.
      p. cm. -- (Basics of the faith)
  Includes bibliographical references.
  ISBN 978-1-59638-430-9 (pbk.)
  1. Christianity--Essence, genius, nature. 2. Faith. I. Title.
  BT60.R57 2012
  234'.23--dc23

                                          2012012422

■ For as far back in my childhood as I can remember, I was always a New Orleans Saints football fan. And for as far back as I can remember, the Saints were always a terrible team. During the first twenty years of the franchise's existence, the team failed to achieve even one winning season. Fans often hung their heads in shame and, at one point, even covered them with brown paper bags. Many went so far as to refer to the team as the "Aints"—instead of the Saints— because of their consistent inability to win football games.

All that changed in 1987, and the last 25 seasons have been much more successful. The Saints even won the Super Bowl in 2010 for the first time and, when they did, thousands of fans exploded onto the streets of New Orleans in celebration. Years of frustration had finally given way to success. Before 1987, however, this kind of success was utterly inconceivable. The team averaged a mere four wins per season. Simply achieving a winning record was a goal that seemed to be beyond their reach.

Sometime before 1987—no doubt in the midst of one of the Saints' more lackluster seasons—I remember seeing a sign appear in the New Orleans Superdome for the first time containing a phrase that has since become quite popular. The sign said, "You just gotta believe!" Even as a young boy, its message was quite clear to me: even though there was no reason whatsoever to believe that our team could ever come together and win football games, we just had to have faith anyway!

As I reflect now, as a Christian, on this phrase and what it communicates about the nature of faith, I cannot help but think that it accurately conveys one of the more popular *mis*understandings of what faith is really all about. I think that many people today, both in the church and in the world, perceive faith as believing when there is absolutely no reason to believe at all. They regard it as a blind leap in the dark or as an irrational feeling of closeness to God. Just like the sign in the Superdome, they think faith means "you just gotta believe!"

FAITH IS INTELLECTUAL

In opposition to this, Reformed Christianity has always maintained that faith is not leaping blindly in the dark or believing for no reason at all, but that it contains an intellectual aspect. The intellectual aspect of faith was so important to the sixteenth-century Reformers and their successors that they tended to define faith in terms of knowledge. Thus, the great Genevan Reformer John Calvin said:

> Faith rests not on ignorance, but on knowledge. And this is, indeed, knowledge not only of God but of the divine will. We do not obtain salvation either because we are prepared to embrace as true whatever the church has prescribed, or because we turn over to it the task of inquiring and knowing. But we [obtain salvation] when we know that God is our merciful Father, because of reconciliation effected

through Christ, and that Christ has been given to us as righteousness, sanctification, and life. By this knowledge, I say, not by submission of our feeling, do we obtain entry into the Kingdom of Heaven.[1]

For Calvin, faith did not consist in a "pious ignorance," or in an "ignorance tempered by humility," or in a "submission of our feeling[s]." Faith, for Calvin, consisted in knowledge—a personal knowledge of God, of Christ, and of the Word.[2]

Almost 100 years later, Samuel Rutherford, the prominent Scottish commissioner to the Westminster Assembly, defined faith in much the same way as did Calvin, calling it an "assurance of knowledge that Christ came into the world to die for sinners."[3] Like Calvin, Rutherford clearly understood that faith must have an intellectual aspect. It must have some kind of doctrinal or factual content. It cannot merely be a feeling or a stubborn commitment devoid of all doctrine. It must *know* certain things. As Alexander Henderson, one of Rutherford's contemporaries at the Westminster Assembly, once said: "an ignorant faith . . . is no faith."[4]

We live in one of the most anti-doctrinal ages in history. As a rule, we do not like doctrine today. We tend either to dismiss it as being irrelevant—just as irrelevant as the longstanding question of how many angels can dance on the head of a pin—or to oppose it outright as that which fosters division and hinders genuine faith and piety. The creed for many well-meaning folks in our day is, "I don't want doctrine; I just want Jesus." And they find their justification for believing this way in passages such as Matthew 18:3, which point to a "childlike" faith as the prerequisite for entering the kingdom of heaven.

What are we to say in response to this? Well, in the first place, although it is true that Jesus does advocate a child*like* faith, he never advocates a child*ish* faith. This is precisely where many Christians get confused. When Jesus states that we must have a childlike faith in order to enter the kingdom of heaven, he means that our faith must be implicitly accepting and trusting—just like a child's. He does not mean that our faith is to be on the intellectual level of a child. This is clear in the many passages of the Bible that advocate maturity in the Christian life and that command us to grow up in our faith (e.g., Heb. 5:11–6:1; Eph. 4:13–16; 1 Cor. 14:20; and 2 Peter 3:18). Faith is certainly to be childlike, but it is never to be childish.

In the second place, the Bible repeatedly emphasizes the importance of doctrine for Christian faith. We see this in passages such as Matthew 22:37 and Romans 12:2, both of which lay stress on the centrality of the mind. But we especially see it in the overwhelming number of passages that speak of the importance of teaching and of sound teaching in particular—e.g., Deuteronomy 4:1; 6:7; 32:44–47; Psalms 25:4–5, 8–9; 119:12, 26, 33, 68; Jeremiah 32:33; Matthew 28:18–20; Acts 2:42; 1 Timothy 1:3–7; 3:2; 4:11–16; 5:17; 6:2–3; Titus 1:9; 2:1; Hebrews 5:11–14.[5]

Two of the passages mentioned above are worth examining in detail. The first, Matthew 28:18–20, is the so-called Great Commission, in which Jesus commands his disciples to go out into the world and make disciples of all nations. The significant thing about this passage is the emphasis that Jesus places on teaching or doctrine in the process of making disciples. It is not by helping others to feel close to God, or by provoking them to take a blind leap in the dark, that Jesus' followers are to make disciples, but *by teaching* them. Doctrine is not irrelevant, for Jesus. Rather, it is the primary means by which men and women will become his followers. To be sure, it can devolve into discussions and arguments about abstruse things. But, in these cases, we need to ensure that we differentiate between doctrine, which is revealed in Scripture either explicitly or by "good and necessary consequence," and opinion, which is not.[6] It may be fun to sit around and argue about the number of angels that can dance on the head of a pin, but in the end we need to remember that Scripture is silent on that matter. And if Scripture is silent, we should be too. According to Jesus, doctrine is not speculative; it is wholly practical and relevant, and it is of primary importance for all who follow him.

The second passage, Acts 2:42, is equally well known and equally significant for its emphasis on teaching. In this passage we are presented with the first glimpse of the post-Pentecost Christian church. The first distinguishing characteristic that we see is not its music or its experiential worship or even its commitment to the extraordinary gifts of the Holy Spirit, but its devotion to the apostles' teaching. This first-order devotion to teaching, however, should not surprise us. We should expect that a church that was established by teaching—à la Matthew 28—would continue to be devoted to that teaching. This is precisely what we do find in Acts 2:42. It would be surprising if it were any other way.

The Bible never advocates a childish faith. Doctrine matters to Jesus and to his followers. We cannot say, "I don't want doctrine; I just want Jesus," because we cannot have Jesus without doctrine. For one thing, how do we know which Jesus it is that we want? There have been thousands of people on earth named Jesus. (There still are quite a few—check any of the team rosters in Major League Baseball!) Which

Jesus is it that we want? <u>Answering that question requires doctrine.</u>

For another thing, Jehovah's Witnesses, Mormons, Christian Scientists, Unitarians, and liberals all believe in Jesus. But they do not believe in the same Jesus that Christians believe in. They do not believe in the Jesus of the Bible. Christian faith must of necessity contain an intellectual aspect. Without it, there is nothing to distinguish the Christian faith from the faith of Jehovah's Witnesses, Mormons, Christian Scientists, Unitarians, and Liberals, on the one hand, or from a sugar high or an adrenaline rush, on the other. Doctrine is not only relevant to the Christian life, it is indispensable. We cannot have Jesus without it. Faith without doctrine is not faith at all but merely a "blind guessing,"[7] as Rutherford says, or a "pious ignorance," as Calvin says. Reformed Christianity has always maintained that genuine faith must, in the first place, involve the knowledge of certain necessary doctrines or facts.[8]

FAITH IS RELATIONAL

Reformed Christianity, however, has also maintained that genuine faith must involve more than just the knowledge of certain doctrines or facts. Faith cannot merely be intellectual. Simply knowing things *about* God is inadequate. Even the demons have this kind of faith (James 2:18–19). Christian faith involves knowing God in relationship. Listen to what the magisterial Reformer Martin Luther said on this point:

> Thus Peter explains it, and correctly so: "Grow in the knowledge of our Lord Jesus Christ" (2 Peter 3:18). . . . This knowledge is faith itself, not only a his-

torical faith, which the devil also has and with which he confesses God as the heretics do, too. It is rather a knowledge which rests on experience, and faith. This word "knowing" means as much as: "Adam knew his wife" (Gen. 4:1), that is, he "knew" her by the sense of feeling, he found her to be his wife, not in a speculative or historical way but by experience.[9]

Knowledge is faith for Luther, as it was for Calvin and Rutherford, and it involves more than simply comprehending certain important facts. It involves an intimate relationship, similar to that of a husband and wife.

The Bible frequently uses the word "knowledge" in this way to refer to an intimate relationship. Perhaps the best-known example of this is found in Jesus' words to his disciples in the Sermon on the Mount (Matt. 7:22–23):

> On that day many will say to me, "Lord, Lord, did we not prophesy in your name, and cast out demons in your name, and do many mighty works in your name?" And then will I declare to them, "I never knew [*ginōskō* in the original Greek] you; depart from me, you workers of lawlessness."[10]

Now, obviously, Jesus did know certain *facts* about these people. He knew enough, for instance, to know that they were "workers of lawlessness." What is more, by way of his omniscience, he knew them better than they knew themselves. Why, then, would Jesus say that he never knew them? Jesus is using the word "know" to mean more than "knowing about"; he is using it to refer to a relationship. Jesus knows them, but he does not have a relationship with them.

Matthew 1:24–25 presents another interesting example for us to consider. In these verses we are told that "Joseph . . . took [Mary as] his wife, but knew [again, *ginōskō* in the Greek] her not until she had given birth to a son . . . Jesus."[11] Here, just as in Luther's example from Genesis 4:1, the word "know" is used to refer to more than an intellectual comprehension of facts. The point is not that Joseph did not know anything at all about Mary, but that he did not consummate his marriage until after Jesus was born. In this case, too, the word "know" refers to the most intimate kind of knowledge that can exist in a relationship.

Many other passages of Scripture explicitly link "knowledge" and "love." They include Genesis 18:19; Exodus 2:25; 33:13, 17; Psalms 1:6; 144:3; Isaiah 43:10; Jeremiah 1:5; Amos 3:2; Hosea 13:5; John 6:69; 10:14–15, 27; 16:3; 17:3; 1 Corinthians 8:3; Galatians 4:9; Philippians 3:8–10; and 2 Timothy 2:19. What this tells us is that faith is more than simply knowing things about Christ. It is loving him and clinging to him with all one's heart. This is why the Belgic Confession (1561) speaks of our need to "embrace Christ."[12] It is also why Samuel Rutherford calls faith a "hanging upon Christ with all the heart for salvation" and a "cleaving" to him with all the heart as though the believer and Christ were "glewed together."[13]

The link between faith and love in Scripture led Rutherford and many other Reformation and post-Reformation theologians to regard marriage-love as the ultimate paradigm to describe the faith relationship between Christ and the individual believer. Just as the husband and wife are commanded to "leave" their parents and to "cleave" to one another in a love relationship (à la Gen. 2:24 and Matt. 19:5), so the Christian is to do the same with Christ. Faith, according to Rutherford, is that which "layeth hold on relations, and such a relation as is betweene husband and wife."[14] Rutherford frequently refers to faith as "marriage-faith" and "marriage-love," and to Christians as those who are "married on Christ" and who "kiss Christ."[15] John Calvin adopts similar language by referring to faith as a "sacred wedlock through which we are made flesh of his flesh and bone of his bone [Eph. 5:30], and thus one with him."[16] And Martin Luther went so far as to say that the faith relationship between Christ and the believer is even stronger than the marriage relationship between husband and wife:

> by [faith] thou art so glewed to Christ, that of thee and Christ, there is as it were *quasi*, made one person, which cannot be segregated, so that with confidence thou may say, I am Christ, that is, Christ's righteousness, victory, and life is mine, and again, *Christ* may say: I am that sinner, that is, his sin and death are mine, because he adhereth to me, and I to him. We are conjoined by faith, in one flesh and bone, *Ephes. 5.*, so that this faith does more nearly couple Christ and me, than the husband to the wife.[17]

The point in all this is simply to say that Reformed Christianity has always understood that saving faith is relational. It involves more than merely knowing facts and doctrines about Christ. It involves knowing Christ himself in relationship—a relationship that is expressed in Scripture in the most intimate of terms.

This Reformed understanding of faith flies in the face of the contemporary "revivalist" view that sees faith in more utilitarian terms, as something like fire insurance. Those who see faith in this way are convinced that it is not relational at all. It is at best a decision that one makes out of prudence or by common sense. But while it may be "good" and "wise" to have fire insurance, it is far more than that to have Christ. John Calvin, Martin Luther, and Samuel Rutherford helpfully remind us that saving faith *cherishes* Christ and "cleaves" to him with all the heart.

We live in a time of great apathy in the church. A recent survey of Christians aged 18 to 29 found that only 15 percent of them could qualify as being "deeply committed." Most of them did not regard their faith as an important part of their lives, and most did not attend church or read their Bibles regularly. The author of the survey, Thom Rainer, drew the conclusion that "most" Christians today—especially in the under-30 age group—"are just indifferent" toward Christ.[18]

One thing the Reformed emphasis on faith as an intimate relationship teaches us is that this kind of indifference has no place in the Christian life. The believer is not indifferent toward Christ; he or she loves Christ. To be sure, this love may start small and grow over the course of the Christian life, and, to some degree, it will wax and wane even as it grows. But it must be there if faith is genuine, and the periods in which the believer's love for Christ wanes ought to be the exception rather than the rule, because, by definition, faith is not apathetic toward Christ but cherishes him. As the English Puritan Walter Marshall says, Christians "are called to enjoy Christ and his salvation more than . . . anything else" and to "reject everything that stands in competition with enjoying Jesus." In the eyes of the genuine believer, Jesus is "distinguished among ten thousand (Song of Songs 5:10),"[19] or, as Rutherford says, the "Chief among ten thousands, the fairest among the sons of men."[20]

One of the other things we learn from the Reformed emphasis on faith as an intimate relationship is that faith is an active and ongoing commitment. This is part and parcel of what it means to be in relationship. By definition, a relationship is not a onetime encounter but an ongoing commitment that requires sustained effort. No marriage can remain strong for very long if the relationship is neglected. The same is true of the faith relationship between Christ and the believer, as Rutherford also pointed out in the seventeenth century:

> Frequent and multiplied acts of marriage-love add a great deal of firmness and of strength to the Marriage band. . . . Renewed acts of faith to take *Christ* for *Jesus* and Redeemer, and renewed acts of love, do more and more engage the heart to *Christ* as Lord and King. Little conversing with *Christ* deadens marriage-love.[21]

Christians can expect their faith to wane to the degree that they neglect their relationship with Christ. Just as "little conversing . . . deadens marriage-love," so little time with Christ in prayer and Bible study produces indifference. Saving faith is a relationship that requires ongoing commitment and sustained effort. We cannot make a onetime decision to "believe" in Christ and then sit on our hands and do nothing, neglecting both Christ and his Word. Faith cherishes Christ and his Word and is committed to doing so.

FAITH IS FIDUCIAL

Faith is not only intellectual and relational, however; it is also fiducial—a word derived from the Latin *fiducia*, meaning "trust." Reformed Christianity has generally believed that saving faith involves not only knowing Christ but also trusting him. According to John Calvin and Samuel Rutherford, this means "resting" or "leaning" on Christ in much the same way as a "weary pilgrim" might rest or lean on "a staff or a rod."[22] Christians are to lean on Christ and not on anything else—i.e., not themselves, not their own abilities or resources, not the government or another person, not even the church (see, e.g., Ps. 71:5–6; Prov. 3:5–6; and Isa. 10:20). They are to entrust their souls and all that they are and have to Christ. They are to look to him (Isa. 45:22; John 6:40; Heb. 12:1–2) as the only basis on which they can be saved and commit themselves to him (Matt. 11:28; 2 Tim. 1:12) as his followers (Matt. 28:18–20; Luke 9:57–62). In the words of the Westminster Confession of Faith (1647), trusting Christ means "accepting, receiving, and resting upon Christ alone for justification, sanctification, and eternal life."[23]

Interestingly, this kind of trust is always built on knowledge. The reason that we trust our physicians, for example, is that we know certain things about them. We know that they have been to medical school, that they have passed the required examinations there, that they are experienced and skilled at what they do, and that they have our best interests in mind. We would not trust just anyone to perform open-heart surgery on us—at least, I hope not. We would want to know certain things first about the surgeon, and then about the nurses, the hospital, and the procedures that would be done. Our trust is built directly on what we know.

Here again we see that faith must necessarily be intellectual. To say that Christian faith is a blind leap in the dark is as absurd as saying that we would walk out onto a busy street and ask the first person we see to perform open-heart surgery on us. That would not be faith; it would be stupidity, plain and simple—along the same lines as blindly leaping off a mountain in the vain hope that there just *might* be a ledge below to save our lives. Christian faith trusts Christ, not because it is a blind leap, but precisely because it knows him.

In an appendix to his book *He is There and He Is Not Silent*, Francis Schaeffer gives a helpful example of what the fiducial aspect of faith looks like in its relationship to knowledge:

> Suppose we are climbing in the Alps and are very high on the bare rock, and suddenly the fog shuts down. The guide turns to us and says that the ice is forming and that there is no hope; before morning we will all freeze to death here on the shoulder of the mountain. Simply to keep warm the guide keeps us moving in the dense fog further out on the shoulder until none of us have any idea where we are. After an hour or so, someone says to the guide, "Suppose I dropped and hit a ledge ten feet down in the fog. What would happen then?" The guide would say that you might make it until the morning and thus live. So, with absolutely no knowledge or any reason to support his action, one of the group hangs and drops into the fog. This would be one kind of faith, a leap of faith.
>
> Suppose, however, after we have worked out on the shoulder in the midst of the fog and the growing ice on the rock, we had stopped and we heard a voice which said, "You cannot see me, but I know exactly where you are from your voices. I am on another ridge. I have lived in these mountains, man and boy, for over sixty years and I know every foot of them. I assure you that ten feet below you there is a ledge.

If you hang and drop, you can make it through the night and I will get you in the morning."

I would not hang and drop at once, but would ask questions to try to ascertain if the man knew what he was talking about and if he was not my enemy. In the Alps, for example, I would ask him his name. If the name he gave me was the name of a family from that part of the mountains, it would count a great deal to me. In the Swiss Alps, there are certain family names that indicate mountain families of that area. In my desperate situation, even though time would be running out, I would ask him what to me would be the adequate and sufficient questions, and when I became convinced by his answers, then I would hang and drop.[24]

Schaeffer's example demonstrates that faith is fiducial; it trusts God, the One who speaks. This trust is not blind. It knows certain facts or doctrines about God, it receives them as good and true, and it is convinced that the One who speaks is trustworthy. Based on all these things, the individual trusts the One who speaks and then acts on that trust by—in the example above—hanging and dropping to the unseen ledge below.

FAITH IS NOT A WORK BUT EXPRESSES ITSELF IN WORK

Schaeffer's example does more than teach that faith is fiducial. It also points to an important feature of the historical Reformed view of faith, namely, that faith is not a work but always expresses itself in work. We will discuss both parts of this statement in turn, beginning with the first part, that faith is not a work, and ending with the second, that faith always expresses itself in work.

In his book *The Tryal and Triumph of Faith*, Samuel Rutherford portrays faith as "a palsied hand under Christ to receive him."[25] By speaking in this way, Rutherford is attempting to emphasize the biblical teaching that faith is a free gift from God and not a meritorious work (Rom. 4:4–5; 6:23; Eph. 2:8–9). As Rutherford sees it, faith cannot be compared to a strong and healthy hand that reaches out and takes hold of Christ for itself, but only to a diseased hand that is capable of doing nothing for itself except receiving what has been placed within its grasp.

J. Gresham Machen makes the same point in his book *What Is Faith?* by appealing to the account of the healing of the centurion's servant in Luke 7:2–10 and Matthew 8:5–13 and saying:

> The point of the narrative is not that [the centurion] did anything, but rather that he did nothing; he simply believed that Jesus could do something, and accepted that thing at Jesus' hands; he simply believed that Jesus could work the stupendous miracle of healing at a distance. In other words, the centurion is presented as one who had faith; and faith, as distinguished from the effects of faith, consists not in doing something but in receiving something.[26]

For Machen, like Rutherford before him, faith does not consist in *doing* anything; it consists in *receiving* everything. Faith is not a work. It does nothing; it offers nothing; it accomplishes nothing; it brings nothing; it earns nothing. It only receives what God freely gives.

But this does not mean that faith is wholly passive. Reformed Christianity has always held, in the first place, that faith itself is active. It knows; it loves; it trusts; it receives. These are all human actions. But they are not meritorious works, because they are all given by the grace of God. [As Rutherford says, "Not only the gift of freely imputed righteousness [i.e., justification], but faith, a mind to believe, sense of poverty, and want of Christ; [and] the actual exercise of faith are all from the free grace of God."[27] Faith is not passive. Each of us must personally appropriate the knowledge of Christ and must choose to love Christ and to put our trust in Christ for ourselves. No one will do these things for us. We must each act for ourselves. But if and when we act, we do so only in response to God's prior work enabling and ensuring all our actions.]

In the second place, Reformed Christianity has always maintained that faith necessarily *expresses* itself in action. Both Martin Luther and John Calvin taught that while good works could not in any way merit salvation, they did prove the genuineness of the individual's faith. It is faith alone that saves us. But the faith that saves us will never be alone; it will always be accompanied by good works. As Luther said: "[It is] not that man is justified before God by works, but that the faith which justifies before God is recognized by the witness of its works."[28] Genuine faith necessarily produces good works in the same way that genuinely healthy trees necessarily produce good fruit. Every healthy tree produces good fruit, and every diseased tree produces bad fruit. The healthy tree is not able to produce bad fruit, and the diseased tree is not able to produce good fruit (see, e.g., Matt. 7:16–18; 12:33–37). Faith, just like the healthy tree, will necessarily express itself in good works.

This relationship between faith and good works has led many in the Reformed tradition to talk about good works as being necessary for salvation—not in the sense that they merit salvation but in the sense that they necessarily accompany saving faith like fruit from the tree. Thus Rutherford could say: "It is not enough that you believe . . . you must also show your faith by good works and prayers, and worshiping of God."[29] And, as we have already seen, he could also say that Christians are responsible to cultivate their "marriage" relationship with Christ by spending time with him in prayer and Bible study. But he was clear that these works in no way merited salvation: "[We] deny a necessity of efficiency in works to deserve salvation, but yield *a necessity of their presence*, that the work of salvation be not hindered."[30]

Prayer, Bible study, and other good works must accompany saving faith, because genuine faith will never be without them. They are as necessary to saving faith as breathing is to life. Listen to J. C. Ryle on this point: "All the children of God on earth are alike in this respect. From the moment there is any life and reality about their religion, they pray. Just as the first sign of life in an infant when born into the world, is the act of breathing, so the first act of men and women when they are born again, is *praying*."[31] Good works are necessary, not because they merit salvation, but because saving faith will never be without them. We are saved by faith alone but not by a faith that is alone.

If we borrow from Francis Schaeffer's example cited above, it is easy to see the activity of faith in both of the aforementioned senses. The climber does not simply receive passively the information provided by the one speaking. He actively engages with the one who speaks, asking him questions and evaluating his answers. The climber also personally appropriates the information for himself and chooses to believe what he is hearing and to trust the one who is speaking. That is faith. The climber's action of hanging and dropping to the ledge below is not faith but the fruit of faith—the proof that genuine faith really does exist. It would make no sense at all for the climber to know that the one who speaks to him is true and trustworthy and yet to refuse to drop down to the ledge. If the climber really knows the one who speaks and is convinced that he is not only speaking the truth but is also trustworthy, then he *will* act. If, on the other hand, he chooses not to drop down to the ledge, the climber would be demonstrating that he does not yet have sufficient knowledge, is not yet convinced, or does not yet trust the one who speaks. In other words, he would be demonstrating by his actions—or, perhaps better, by the lack thereof—that he does not yet have faith in the one who speaks.

FAITH IS NOT NECESSARILY STRONG

While faith must be intellectual, relational, fiducial, and active in order to be genuine, it does not necessarily have to be strong or mature. Faith can be weak or small and still be saving faith. The thief on the cross proves this. His faith was clearly not a mature faith, but it was a saving faith nonetheless. The thief knew certain things about God, Christ, and himself; he embraced Christ and trusted in him; and he demonstrated the fact that he possessed saving faith by his actions before he died (Luke 23:39–43).

The example of Abraham further substantiates the fact that faith can be imperfect and yet still be genuine. In Genesis 15:6, Abraham is declared to be in right standing with God—a gift that he receives by faith alone.[32] But the very next thing we see is that Abraham demonstrates a lack of trust in God by seeking to take matters into his own hands and to bring about God's promises by his own initiative (Gen. 16). The faith by which Abraham received God's gift of justification was, thus, an imperfect faith.

We all know the story of Abraham's great faith in Genesis 22, the account in which Abraham is asked to sacrifice his son—the very son through whom God had promised to make him the father of many nations. We all know that Abraham did what God asked him to do and that it was only because God stayed Abraham's hand that the planned sacrifice was not carried out. Abraham really was a man of tremendous faith, more faith than many of us probably will ever have today. I shudder to think how I would respond if God were to ask me to sacrifice my son. That is why I am deeply grateful that Genesis 15:6 does not occur in Genesis 21 or 23. If Genesis 15:6 did occur in one of those later chapters, it would tell us that the kind of faith by which Abraham was justified was a Genesis 22 faith, which is obviously a very deep and mature faith. I am much more thankful that Genesis 15:6 occurs where it does because it tells us that the kind of faith by which Abraham was justified was a Genesis 16 faith—an imperfect and weak faith. I find that to be incredibly encouraging.

As a pastor, I have seen many people struggle to understand how much faith is required in order to be saved. I have seen many outwardly fruitful, obedient Christians struggle with knowing whether or not their faith is genuine, simply because it is not as strong as they think saving faith should be. I have seen others in the wake of the death of a loved one struggle with knowing whether their loved one really believed, simply because there was little visible fruit in the loved one's life. We all know that the Bible is clear in its teaching that faith alone saves us. But the Bible is nowhere near as clear about *how much* faith is required to be a saving faith. As a result, many Christians struggle profoundly.

Personally and pastorally, I have found help in Jesus' words in Matthew 17:20—a passage that I am convinced teaches that saving faith can be quite small and yet still be genuine. In Matthew 17:20, Jesus responds to his disciples' question about why they had failed to cast out a demon from an epileptic boy by saying: "Because of your little faith. For truly, I say to you, if you have faith like a grain of mustard seed, you will say to this mountain, 'Move from here to there,' and it will move, and nothing will be impossible for you." Whatever else Jesus may be saying in this passage, he is at least saying that the disciples—who were obviously not unbelievers—failed to heal the epileptic boy because of their "little faith." In the words of Matthew Henry: "Though they had faith, yet that faith was weak and ineffectual."[33] In and of itself this should be enough to encourage those of us who are struggling. The disciples, like Abraham and the thief on the cross, had a faith that was clearly not invincible. It was weak and altogether imperfect, but it was sufficient to number them among the redeemed.

But there is more in this passage for us to see. If we use Jesus' comments in Matthew 13:31–32 as a guide in understanding what he means in 17:20 when he compares faith to "a grain of mustard seed," the very least we can say is that Jesus believed that it is possible for faith to be quite small and still be saving faith. The mustard seed was commonly known to be the smallest garden seed in the ancient Near East.[34] Whether or not it stayed that way is unimportant at this point. What is important is that in Jesus' mind, it was distinctly possible for faith to be very small—the size of a mustard seed—and still be a genuine, saving faith.

Martin Luther emphasized the smallness of saving faith in the sixteenth century when he said:

> He who has fallen into a river probably grasps the branch of a tree by which he barely keeps himself from perishing. So we, too, apprehend Christ in the midst of sins, in death and distress, with a faith that is weak. And yet faith, however small it may be, saves us, rules over death, and treads the devil and all underfoot.[35]

John Calvin also repeatedly pointed out that genuine faith is oftentimes "tinged with doubt" and "assailed by some anxiety."[36] It is not a perfect faith, a mature faith, or a strong faith that wins the victory and receives the gift of eternal life but a weak and small faith, a faith that is much more like a palsied hand than a healthy, vibrant one. It is not the *quantity* or *quality* of the individual's faith that matters so much as the *reality* of it.

Sometimes I think that we forget this as Christians. We forget that faith is oftentimes weak and small, especially when it is first expressed. We look for a mature faith in ourselves or in others and frequently use that as our standard for judging. We quickly label others as non-Christians, or we struggle with assurance of salvation ourselves, precisely because we are looking for perfection or for maturity rather than for the presence of saving faith, no matter how small. Reformed Christianity, however, has always held that faith does not need to be strong or mature; it needs only to be real or genuine.

But just because faith does not have to be strong or mature, that does not mean it should *always* be small or weak. Genuine faith may start out small or weak, but it does not stay that way. Saving faith grows and matures. It grows in its knowledge, in its love, in its ability to trust, and in its fruitfulness. We saw this earlier when we showed that faith is not child*ish* but child*like*. Saving faith is intellectual; it knows about Christ, and it grows in its knowledge. Saving faith is relational; it knows Christ in relationship, and this relationship grows and deepens and matures. Saving faith is fiducial; it trusts Christ and grows in its ability to trust him with all that we are and have. Saving faith is active; it embraces Christ, produces works of obedience in keeping with it, and grows in its fruitfulness. And saving faith is not necessarily strong or mature in its expression; it is oftentimes weak and small, like a grain of mustard seed. But it does not remain this way. It grows and matures, just as the mustard seed does not remain a seed but grows into mature adulthood.

What is faith? Faith is *knowing* Christ, *loving* Christ, and *trusting* Christ in a way that is both active and growing. It is not leaping blindly in the dark or believing for no reason at all, because faith has an intellectual component. It is not a wholly rational exercise of the mind or an apathetic acquiescence, because faith has a relational component. It is not self-reliance or inactivity but always leads to obedience and the bearing of much fruit, because faith is fiducial and active. And it is not perfect or stagnant, because faith begins small and grows over the course of the believer's life. Faith knows; faith loves; faith trusts; faith acts; and faith grows. This is the kind of faith that receives God's free gift of eternal life. Without it, none of us will enter the kingdom of heaven. In that sense—and only in that sense—is it true that "you just gotta believe!"

NOTES

1 John Calvin, *Institutes of the Christian Religion*, ed. John T. McNeill, trans. Ford Lewis Battles (Philadelphia: Westminster, 1960), 3.2.2.

2 Ibid., 3.2.2–3 and 3.2.6–7.

3 Samuel Rutherford, *Ane Catachisme Conteining the Soume of Christian Religion*, in Alexander F. Mitchell, ed., *Catechisms of the Second Reformation* (London: James Nisbet, 1886), 203, with spelling updated.

4 Alexander Henderson, *Sermons, Prayers, and Pulpit Addresses*, ed. R. Thomson Martin (Edinburgh: John Maclaren, 1867), 113, with spelling updated.

5 Our English word "doctrine" comes from the Latin *doctrina*, which means "teaching" or "instruction."

6 See the Westminster Confession of Faith, §1.6.

7 Rutherford, *Catachisme*, 203, with spelling updated.

8 The best-known Reformed confessions teach that faith contains the intellectual aspect of knowledge—e.g., the Belgic Confession (1561), the Heidelberg Catechism (1563), the Second Helvetic Confession (1566), and the Westminster Confession of Faith (1647), and Shorter (1647) and Larger (1648) Catechisms. See Joel R. Beeke and Sinclair B. Ferguson, eds., *Reformed Confessions Harmonized* (Grand Rapids: Baker, 1999), 94–97.

9 Martin Luther, *Luther's Werke* (Weimar edition), 40 III, 737ff; cited in Ewald M. Plass, comp., *What Luther Says: A Practical In-Home Anthology for the Active Christian* (St. Louis: Concordia Publishing House, 1959), 470.

10 Jesus says the same thing again in the Parable of the Ten Virgins in Matt. 25:12.

11 See also Luke 1:34; Gen. 4:17, 25; and 1 Sam. 1:19.

12 See the Belgic Confession of Faith, Article 22, cited in Beeke and Ferguson, eds., *Reformed Confessions Harmonized*, 94.

13 Rutherford, *Catachisme*, 203; also Samuel Rutherford, *The Covenant of Life Opened* (Edinburgh, 1654), 161.

14 Samuel Rutherford, *A Sermon Preached before the Right Honorable House of Lords* (London, 1645), 50.

15 Rutherford, *Covenant of Life Opened*, 351; Samuel Rutherford, *A Survey of the Spirituall AntiChrist* (London, 1648), 126–28; Rutherford, *A Sermon before the House of Lords*, 48, 50; Samuel Rutherford, *Letters of Samuel*

Rutherford, ed. A. A. Bonar (Edinburgh and London: Oliphant Anderson & Ferrier, 1891), 71, 82, 97–98, 137.

16 Calvin, *Institutes*, 3.1.3.

17 Here Rutherford is quoting Luther with approval (Rutherford, *Spirituall AntiChrist*, 126). Rutherford cites Luther in Latin and then translates him into English. It is this English translation that is cited above.

18 Cathy Lynn Grossman, "Young Adults Less Devoted to Faith," *USA Today*, April 27, 2010, accessed October 12, 2011, www.usatoday.com /printedition/news/20100427/1amillfaith27_st.art.htm.

19 Walter Marshall, *The Gospel Mystery of Sanctification: Growing in Holiness by Living in Union with Christ, A New Version, Put Into Modern English by Bruce H. McRae* (Eugene, OR: Wipf & Stock, 2005), 159.

20 The emphasis on faith as an intimate relationship between the believer and Christ is a theme of Rutherford's *Letters* and a chief reason why they have been treasured by Christians in every generation since their original publication in 1664. In his *Letters*, Rutherford repeatedly refers to Christ with terms of endearment that are reflective of the husband-wife relationship. See, e.g., Rutherford, *Letters*, 78, 89, 106, 137, 184, 254, 309, 446, 556, 637.

21 Rutherford, *Covenant of Life Opened*, 351, with spelling updated.

22 See Calvin, *Institutes*, 3.2.1; 3.2.7; and the current author's discussion in *The Supremacy of God in the Theology of Samuel Rutherford* (Milton Keynes, UK: Paternoster, 2008), 187–88.

23 The Westminster Confession of Faith, §14.2.

24 Francis A. Schaeffer, *He Is There and He Is Not Silent*, in *The Complete Works of Francis A. Schaeffer: A Christian Worldview*, vol. 1 (Wheaton, IL: Crossway, 1982), 351–52.

25 Samuel Rutherford, *The Tryal and Triumph of Faith* (London: 1645), 59, with spelling updated.

26 J. Gresham Machen, *What Is Faith?* (1925; Grand Rapids: Eerdmans, 1962), 88–89.

27 Rutherford, *Spirituall AntiChrist*, II, 114, with spelling updated.

28 Plass, comp., *What Luther Says*, 493. See also Calvin, *Institutes*, 3.16.1.

29 Rutherford, *Fourteen Communion Sermons*, ed. A. A. Bonar (Glasgow: Glass & Co., 1877), 256, with spelling and language updated.

30 Rutherford, *Covenant of Life Opened*, 154, with spelling updated. Calvin went so far as to call good works "inferior causes" of the possession of salvation. But he plainly locates the "efficient cause" or "true cause" in God's mercy alone and not in our works. See Calvin, *Institutes*, 3.14.21.

31 J. C. Ryle, *Practical Religion* (1878; Edinburgh: Banner of Truth, 1998), 65.

32 Cf. Paul's use of Abraham and this verse in Romans 4.

33 Matthew Henry, *Matthew Henry's Commentary on the Whole Bible*, unabridged, vol. 5, Matthew 17:20, accessed April 29, 2011, www.ccel.org/ccel/henry/mhc.i.html.

34 See Roland K. Harrison, "Mustard," in *The International Standard Bible Encyclopedia*, vol. 3, ed. Geoffrey W. Bromiley (Grand Rapids: Eerdmans, 1986), 449. Commentators attest that it was commonly used proverbially to signify a small size, quantity, or weight—at least initially. See, e.g., William Hendriksen, *Exposition of the Gospel According to Matthew*, in *New Testament Commentary* (Grand Rapids: Baker, 1973), 565; and John Gill, *Exposition of the Entire Bible*, Matthew 13:32 and 17:20, accessed October 14, 2011, www.freegrace.net/gill.

35 Plass, comp., *What Luther Says*, 488.

36 Calvin, *Institutes*, 3.2.17.

MORE APOLOGETICS FROM
P&R PUBLISHING

Many question whether the Bible deserves to be called *the* Book or whether it is just *a* book—a very special book, to be sure, but not the Book that perfectly illumines all things. And the more they chip away at the full confidence that believers must have in the trustworthiness of Scripture, the more they rob its Author of the glory that his Word displays and demands.

What's worse is that more and more of these attacks are coming from those who claim to be believers themselves.

Here the Philadelphia Conference on Reformed Theology explores the Author's glory by unfolding the richness and perfection of the Bible. In essays collected from the best addresses on the subject, eight of the top pastor-scholars of the past thirty years share their insight and answers.

MORE WORLDVIEW RESOURCES FROM P&R PUBLISHING

Like it or not, notice it or not, popular culture plays a huge role in our day-to-day lives, influencing the way we think and see the world. Some people respond by trying to pull away from it altogether, and some accept it without question as a blessing. But Ted Turnau reminds us that the issue is not so black-and-white.

Popular culture, like any other facet of society, is a messy mixture of both grace *and* idolatry, and it deserves our serious attention and discernment. Learn how to approach popular culture wisely, separating its gems of grace from its temptations toward idolatry, and practice some *pop*ologetics to be an influence of your own.

"Ted Turnau does a great service toward helping Christians engage their culture with both conviction and open-mindedness . . . and offers excellent practical application for how to both appreciate pop culture and fairly critique it."

—**Brian Godawa**, Hollywood screenwriter,
author of *Hollywood Worldviews*

MORE BIBLICAL INSIGHTS FROM P&R PUBLISHING

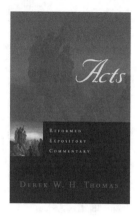

We face relentless opposition as our postmodern world mirrors the world of the apostles. Planting and growing churches in such an environment poses particular challenges. Nevertheless, Acts clearly demonstrates that no obstacle can withstand the power of the Holy Spirit. As he did in the early church, the Holy Spirit teaches us in Acts to "expect great things."

"With pastoral care and thoughtful scholarship, Thomas gets to the very heart of Acts. . . . A much-needed resource for believers of all ages who desire to more fully know God's sovereign history in the early church."
— **Burk Parsons**, editor of *Tabletalk* magazine, minister of congregational life at Saint Andrew's, Sanford, Florida

"Biblically thorough, theologically accurate, pastorally sensitive— here is a rich feast set before God's people. As Derek Thomas feeds us from the book of Acts, not only do we find ourselves satisfied, we are compelled to love Jesus more today than we did yesterday."
— **Sean Michael Lucas**, senior minister, First Presbyterian Church, Hattiesburg, Mississippi